LAUGH
-OUT-
LOUD

THE
1,001 FUNNIEST
LOL JOKES
OF ALL TIME

LAUGH
-OUT-
LOUD

THE
1,001 FUNNIEST
LOL JOKES
OF ALL TIME

ROB ELLIOTT

HARPER
An Imprint of HarperCollinsPublishers

Library of Congress Control Number: 2021935319
ISBN 978-0-06-325563-0

22 23 24 25 26 PC/LSCH 10 9 8 7 6 5 4 3 2 1

First Edition

Q: What did one marshmallow say to the other?

A: "I want s'more time with you!"

Q: How did the zookeeper calm down the wild elephant?

A: With a trunk-quilizer.

Q: Why were there lizards all over the bathroom wall?

A: Because it had been rep-tiled.

Q: Why did the man cry when he ran out of cola?

A: Because it was soda-pressing.

Q: How are bus drivers like trees?

A: They both have routes.

Q: Why did the clock go on vacation?

A: It needed to unwind.

Q: What does a duck wear to its wedding?

A: A ducks-edo!

Q: What does a Tyrannosaurus rex eat while it's camping?

A: Dino-s'mores!

Q: Why did the bee marry the rabbit?

A: She was his honey bunny.

Q: What do sheep always take on camping trips?

A: Their baa-ckpacks.

Q: What do you call a squid with only six arms?

A: A hexa-pus.

Q: Why can't you take a skunk on vacation?

A: Your trip will stink!

Q: What do you call the worm that ate Beethoven?

A: A de-composer.

Q: Why should you always listen to porcupines?

A: They have a lot of good points.

Q: What do you get when you cross a carrot and a pair of scissors?

A: Par-snips.

Q: Why don't sand dollars take baths?

A: Because they wash up on the shore.

Q: Why did the boy and girl play tennis on their date?

A: It was a court-ship.

Andy: Did you hear about the panther that told the boy he wouldn't eat him?

Daniel: No, what happened?

Andy: He was lion.

Q: Why did the butcher work so hard?

A: He had to bring home the bacon.

Q: What goes up and down but never moves?

A: A flight of stairs.

Q: How much does it cost to become an electrician?

A: There's no charge.

Q: How do crabs buy their toys?

A: With sand dollars.

Q: What kind of pole can't you climb?

A: A tadpole.

Q: Why wouldn't the jellyfish go down the water slide?

A: Because he was spineless.

Q: How did the farmer show his wife he loved her?

A: He brought home the bacon.

Q: What does a trash collector eat for lunch?

A: Junk food.

Q: **What did the man do when he was standing out in a thunderstorm?**

A: He hailed a cab.

Q: **Why did the mummy keep hugging her kids goodbye?**

A: She thought they were eerie-sistible.

Q: **Do turkeys like to eat hot lunch?**

A: Yes, they gobble it right up.

Q: **What do spiders eat at a picnic?**

A: Corn on the cobweb.

Q: Why was the butterfly embarrassed when it came to the dance?

A: Because it was a moth ball.

Q: What happened when the beagle played in the snow?

A: It turned into a chili dog!

Q: How do gardeners kiss?

A: With their tulips.

Q: Why wouldn't the cow get a job?

A: Because he was a meat loafer.

Q: What do you get if you put a pig on a racetrack?

A: A road hog!

Q: What do you call a crocodile that's always picking fights?

A: An insti-gator.

Q: What do whales eat for a snack?

A: Ships and salsa.

Q: Where does a sailor go when he's sick?

A: To the dock.

Q: Why did the robin get a library card?

A: It was hoping to find some bookworms.

Q: Why did the pilot paint his jet?

A: He thought it was too plane.

Q: What did the girl snake say to the boy snake?

A: "Will you be my boa-friend?"

Q: How do artists get to work?

A: They go over the drawbridge.

Q: Where do tarantulas get their information?

A: From the World Wide Web.

Q: Why do cows believe everything you say?

A: Because they're so gulli-bull.

Q: What's a pirate's favorite subject?

A: Arrr-ithmetic.

Q: Why did the whale buy a violin?

A: So it could join the orca-stra.

Q: What kind of bugs weigh less every day?

A: Lightening bugs.

Q: Why did the meteorite go to Hollywood?

A: It wanted to be a star.

Q: Why don't polar bears and penguins fall in love?

A: Because they're polar opposites.

Q: What do you call a hamburger in space?

A: A meat-eor!

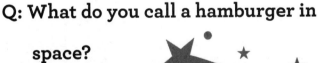

Luke: I'm so tired of climbing this big hill!

Zack: Oh, get over it!

Q: Why don't turtles use the drive-through?

A: They don't like fast food.

Q: How do the basketball players stay cool during games?

A: They sit by their fans.

Q: Where do elephants keep their spare tires?

A: In their trunks.

Q: What falls down but never gets hurt?

A: Raindrops!

Q: How did the lettuce win the race?

A: It got a head start!

Q: What happened when the vampire met his blind date?

A: It was love at first bite.

Q: Why didn't the melons get married?

A: Because they cantaloupe.

Q: What kind of shoes do ninjas wear?

A: Sneakers.

Q: How does Saturn clean its rings?

A: With a meteor shower!

Q: What is the best way to get straight A's in school?

A: Use a ruler.

Q: When do scuba divers sleep underwater?

A: When they're snore-kling.

Q: Why wouldn't the earthworm play outside?

A: It was grounded.

Q: Why did the mechanic stop pumping gas?

A: It was a tank-less job.

Q: Why shouldn't you date a sausage?

A: Because they're the wurst!

Q: What's a tornado's favorite game?

A: Twister!

Q: How did the monkey escape from the zoo?

A: In a hot-air baboon.

Q: What is something you always leave behind at the beach?

A: Your footprints.

Q: Why did the textbook go to the hospital?

A: It needed its appendix taken out.

Q: How are flowers like the letter *A*?

A: Bees come after them.

Q: What does a wasp wear when it's raining?

A: A yellow jacket.

Q: Why do dogs have a great attitude?

A: They like to stay paws-itive.

Q: Why did the turtle have a bad time with her date?

A: He wouldn't come out of his shell.

Q: What kind of bugs like sushi?

A: Wasa-bees.

Q: **Why did the pelican run out of money?**

A: It had a big bill.

Q: **What did the ocean do when the kids left the beach?**

A: It waved goodbye.

Q: **Why did the library book go to the chiropractor?**

A: It needed its spine adjusted.

Q: **Why do sharks swim in salt water?**

A: Pepper water makes them sneeze!

Q: **Why do potatoes make good detectives?**

A: They keep their eyes peeled.

Q: **What do they eat in the Navy?**

A: Submarine sandwiches.

Q: **What did the snakes do after their fight?**

A: They hissed and made up.

Q: **Why do wasps need to go on vacation?**

A: Because they're always busy bees.

Q: How do you make a strawberry shake?

A: Tell it a scary story.

Q: Why did the surfer go to the hair salon?

A: She wanted a permanent wave.

Q: Why are clarinet players so smart?

A: Because they reed a lot!

Q: What's a frog's favorite kind of music?

A: Hip-hop!

Q: **How does a bison pay for dinner and a movie?**

A: It uses buffalo bills.

Q: **What do you get when you cross a strawberry with a propeller?**

A: A jelly-copter!

Q: **What do you get when a butcher and a baker get married?**

A: Meat loaf.

Q: **What do you get when you cross a king with a boat?**

A: Leadership!

Q: **Why did the berry go out with the fig?**

A: Because it couldn't get a date.

Tom: **Hey, want to hear another insect joke?**

Jim: No, stop bugging me!

Rita: **Do you know where they cooked the first French fries?**

Stephanie: France?

Rita: **No, in Greece!**

Sam: **Why did the alien grow a garden in space?**

Marcus: It had a green thumb!

Q: What do you call it when two boats fall in love?

A: A relation-ship.

Q: Why is it hard to be a firefighter?

A: You get fired every day!

Q: How do mountains stay warm in the winter?

A: With their snowcaps.

Q: How do you send a knight on a mission?

A: You give him a re-quest.

Q: **Why wouldn't the acrobat perform in winter?**

A: He only knew how to do summer-saults.

Q: **How do bees fix their hair?**

A: With a honey-comb.

Q: **What do you get when you cross a crocodile and a GPS?**

A: A navi-gator.

Q: Why were the goats sent to the principal's office?

A: They kept butting heads.

Q: What is a beluga's favorite drink?

A: Mana-tea.

Q: Where do tarantulas look for love?

A: On dating web-sites.

Q: Where do pirates go to the bathroom?

A: On the poop deck.

Q: How did the polar bear get to work?

A: On a motor-icicle.

Q: Why did the beaver cross the road?

A: To get to the otter side.

Q: What goes up when the rain comes down?

A: An umbrella.

Q: What happens when a toad is nervous?

A: It gets worry warts!

Q: Why did the chicken run onto the soccer field?

A: Because the ref called fowl.

Q: How do fish get around the busy ocean?

A: They hail a crab.

Q: What did the stamp say to the envelope?

A: "I'm stuck on you."

Q: Why did the lumberjack fall asleep?

A: He was board!

Q: **What do you get when your dad rides a bike?**

A: A pop-cycle.

Q: **Why was the tightrope walker stressed out?**

A: He was having trouble balancing his schedule.

Q: **What kind of bow can't you tie?**

A: A rainbow.

Q: **What do you get when you cross a cow with a roll of tape?**

A: A beef stick.

Q: **Why don't bumblebees drink coffee before they go to school?**

A: They get too buzzed!

Q: **How does the sun kiss the moon?**

A: It puckers its ec-lipse.

Q: **Why did the noses break up?**

A: They kept picking on each other.

Q: **What do you call tiny glasses?**

A: Speck-tacles.

Q: **What do you call a dancing sheep?**

A: A baaa-llerina.

Q: When is a boxer a comedian?

A: When he delivers a punch line!

Q: Why did the skunk become a police officer?

A: It believed in law and odor.

Q: Why do skunks always show off?

A: They want to be the scent-er of attention.

Q: What do groundhogs like to read?

A: Pop-up books.

Q: What kind of bird do you send on a quest?

A: A knight owl.

Q: Why did the meteorologist cancel her date?

A: She was feeling under the weather.

Q: What do you get when you throw cabbage in the snow?

A: Cold slaw.

Q: Why did the cow become an acrobat?

A: It was so flexi-bull!

Q: What do you get when a witch loses her magic?

A: A hex-a-gone.

Q: What do you call an angry vegetable?

A: A grum-pea!

Q: Why don't canaries want to pay for a vacation?

A: Because they're cheep!

Q: Why did the librarian wear sparkly purple glasses?

A: She wanted to make a spectacle of herself.

Q: What kind of lion can you let in the house?

A: A dande-lion!

Q: How did the broom know it was in love?

A: It was swept off its feet.

Q: Where do you take a fish for an operation?

A: To the sturgeon.

Q: Where do tropical fish keep their work?

A: In a reef-case.

Q: What do you eat for lunch in the desert?

A: Sand-wiches.

Q: Where do trees go when they are tired?

A: For-rest.

Q: What goes tick, tick, woof, woof?

A: A watchdog.

Q: Where do they make all the books for school?

A: In a fact-ory.

Q: **What do you get when you combine a snail and a porcupine?**

A: A slowpoke!

Q: **What happened to the atoms when they got in fight?**

A: They split up!

Q: **What happens if a kangaroo can't jump?**

A: It feels un-hoppy.

Q: **What do bananas and acrobats have in common?**

A: They can both do splits.

Q: When can't you trust a painter?

A: When he's a con artist.

Q: What kinds of birds are never happy?

A: Bluebirds.

Q: Why didn't the man trust his bushes?

A: They seemed shady.

Q: Why was the nose feeling sad at school?

A: It kept getting picked on.

Q: What kind of candy do boxers eat?

A: Jawbreakers!

Q: Why did the tailor and the quilter get married?

A: Because they were sew in love!

Susie: Want to go see the llamas?

Sofia: That sounds fun!

Susie: Alpaca suitcase.

Q: Why can't you give your dog the TV remote?

A: It'll keep hitting the paws button.

Q: How does a slug cross the ocean?

A: In a snailboat!

Q: When is a snail the life of the party?

A: When it comes out of its shell.

Q: What happened when the duck went to the doctor?

A: It got a clean bill of health.

Q: What do sea turtles like to study?

A: Current events.

Q: Why is it hard to beat a barber in a race?

A: They take shortcuts!

Q: Why do baseball players always take their dates to restaurants?

A: They like to stay behind the plate.

Q: Where does a rabbit go when he needs glasses?

A: A hop-thalmologist.

Q: Why did the snail take a nap?

A: It was feeling sluggish.

Q: **When do bees keep you healthy?**

A: When they're vitamin B's.

Q: **Where does a peach take a nap?**

A: On an apri-cot.

Q: **Why did the student throw the calendar out the window?**

A: To make the days fly by.

Q: **What do boxers eat for dinner?**

A: Black-eyed peas.

Q: **What do you call a sleepy woodcutter?**

A: A slumber-jack.

Q: What kind of dog is always sad?

A: A melon-collie.

Q: What did the horse say when its date didn't show up for dinner?

A: "That's the last straw!"

Q: What kind of bread is the cheapest?

A: Pumper-nickel.

Q: Why do seeds make great friends?

A: They're always rooting for you!

Q: What kind of cheese stays by itself?

A: Prov-alone.

Q: What is the difference between students and fish?

A: Students love Fridays and fish hate fry-days!

Q: What do you call a cow with a telescope?

A: A star grazer.

Jim: I want to canoe down the river today.

Sue: You otter do that!

Q: What do clowns eat for lunch?

A: Peanut butter and jolly sandwiches.

Q: Why was the climbing rope anxious?

A: It was getting all strung out!

Q: What do a dog and a watch have in common?

A: They both have ticks.

Q: What kind of vegetable is hot and cold at the same time?

A: A chilly pepper.

Q: What did the hen say to its chick?

A: "You're a good egg."

Q: Why did the farmer study geometry?

A: He already had a pro-tractor!

Q: What do TVs wear to the beach?

A: Sun-screen.

Q: What do you call two birds in love?

A: Tweet-hearts.

Q: What's a bunny's favorite toy?

A: A hula hop.

Q: Why was the scuba diver embarrassed?

A: He saw the ocean's bottom.

Q: What's a farmer's favorite movie?

A: Beauty and the Beets.

Q: Why did the bee go to the allergist?

A: It had hives.

Q: What do you call songs you compose in bed?

A: Sheet music.

Q: Why did the thermometer go back to college?

A: It wanted another degree.

Q: Why did the shark cross the road?

A: To get to the other tide.

Q: What did one leaf say to the other leaf?

A: "I think I'm falling for you."

Q: Why did the butcher follow the detective?

A: He wanted to go on a steak-out.

Q: Why wouldn't the chicken grow?

A: It had smallpox.

Q: What did the dog have to do before going out to play?

A: Ask its paw first.

Q: How does a boy let you know he called?

A: He leaves a voice male.

Q: Why did the pineapple cake turn upside down?

A: It saw the cinnamon roll!

Q: Why can't you take your hamster to school?

A: They don't make backpacks that small.

Hannah: There's an octopus in my bathtub!

Olivia: You're just squid-ing me!

Q: What did the baker say on her wedding day?

A: "I loaf you with all my heart!"

Q: What do you give a farmer who sings out of tune?

A: A pitchfork.

Q: Why couldn't the oyster talk?

A: It clammed up!

Q: What is a penguin's favorite vegetable?

A: Snow peas.

Q: Why was the cook fired from the sandwich shop?

A: He couldn't cut the mustard!

Amy: What kind of nut do you like in your trail mix?

Susy: Cashew.

Amy: Bless you!

Laura: My pickles won a blue ribbon at the fair!

Mary: That's a very big dill!

Q: What did one magnet say to the other magnet?

A: "I'm very attracted to you!"

Q: What is a shark's favorite game show?

A: Whale of Fortune.

Q: Why did the baker become an actor?

A: He wanted to play a roll.

Q: Why did the vampire join the circus?

A: He wanted to be an acro-bat.

Q: Why can't a scarecrow be a comedian?

A: Its jokes are too corny.

Joe: Why did you put a kazoo in your lunch box?

Jim: I wanted a hum sandwich!

Q: Why didn't Jenny go to the library?

A: She was already booked!

Q: Why did the monkey need some R & R?

A: He was going bananas!

Q: How did the fisherman meet new people?

A: He net-worked.

Q: What is the richest bird?

A: An ost-rich.

Paul: Do you want to try fencing with me?

Pete: I'll take a stab at it.

Q: What is a plumber's favorite vegetable?

A: A leek!

Q: What did the alien say to the soda?

A: "Take me to your liter."

Q: Why couldn't Jake join the track team?

A: There were too many hurdles.

Q: What do you call a polar bear that makes coffee?

A: A bear-ista.

Q: **What did the cheese say to his bride?**

A: "I want to grow mold together."

Q: **How did the flea get from one dog to the other?**

A: It itch-hiked!

Q: **How does a polar bear build its house?**

A: Igloos it together.

Q: **Why can't a giraffe's tongue be twelve inches long?**

A: Because then it would be a foot!

Q: Why was the strawberry stressed out?

A: It was in a jam!

Q: What do you get if your dad gets stuck in the freezer?

A: A Pop-sicle.

Q: What do cows like to play at recess?

A: Dodge-bull.

Q: What is the noisiest animal to own?

A: A trum-pet!

Q: What did the boa constrictor say to the mouse?

A: "I think I have a crush on you!"

Q: What did the star say to the moon?

A: "I'm falling for you!"

Q: Why did the lumberjack get fired?

A: He axed too many questions.

Q: When is your mother like a window?

A: When she's being trans-parent.

Q: Why did the grape go to bed?

A: It ran out of juice!

Q: Why should you keep a whale happy?

A: If it's sad, it'll start blubbering.

Q: What do conductors and mountain climbers have in common?

A: They both like the terrain.

Q: Why did the criminal duck?

A: The judge said he was going to throw the book at him!

Q: What do rabbits play at recess?

A: Hopscotch.

Q: Why was the girl jump-roping down the hall?

A: She was skipping class.

Q: What did the apple say to the banana?

A: "I think you're ap-peeling!"

Q: When does a gorilla put on a suit?

A: When it's got monkey business!

Q: What is the most famous kind of drink?

A: A celebri-tea!

Q: What is a hippo's favorite vegetable?

A: Zoo-cchini.

Q: Why do melons stay single?

A: Because they cantaloupe.

Q: What vegetable do they serve in prison?

A: Cell-ery.

Q: What is the smartest state in America?

A: Alabama, because it has four A's and a B.

Q: Why did the deer get a job?

A: It wanted to make a quick buck.

Q: Why did the collie break up with the German shepherd?

A: It wanted to paws from dating for a while.

Q: What happened when the witch lost control of her broom?

A: She flew off the handle.

Q: How did the fisherman finish in half the time?

A: He was e-fish-ent!

Q: Why did the trombone player try to play his friend's trumpet?

A: His teacher said it's rude to toot your own horn!

Q: What don't grizzlies wear shoes?

A: They like to go bear-foot.

Q: Why did the student bring his stilts to school?

A: For show and tall.

Q: Why was the weatherman so upset?

A: Somebody stole his thunder.

Q: **Why did the slug break up with the snail?**

A: The relationship was moving too slow.

Q: **Why will a squirrel always keep a secret?**

A: It's a tough nut to crack!

Q: **How do snowmen stay warm at night?**

A: With a blanket of snow.

James: Did you hear the joke about the hot-air balloon?

Jack: It went right over my head!

Q: Why did the cucumber call for help?

A: It was in a pickle.

Q: Why did the boy call the fire department?

A: His money was burning a hole in his pocket!

Q: Where do cows eat their lunch?

A: In the calf-eteria.

Q: Why didn't the corn take a plane?

A: Its ears would pop!

Q: Why did the candies fall in love?

A: They were mint for each other.

Q: What do you do if your walls are cold?

A: Put on another coat of paint!

Q: What do you get if you put coffee on your head?

A: A cap-puccino.

Q: What does a queen wear in a thunderstorm?

A: A reign-coat!

Tailor: Do you like your new suit?

Customer: It's sew-sew.

Q: Why did the captain quit her job?

A: Because her ship came in.

Q: Why was the clock looking forward to spring break?

A: It needed to unwind.

Q: Why don't snakes know how much they weigh?

A: They're always losing their scales.

Q: What did the boy cat say to the girl cat?

A: "We're purr-fect for each other!"

Q: Why did the man put his car in the oven?

A: He wanted to drive a hot rod.

Q: How do you fix a broken vegetable?

A: With tomato paste.

Q: What did the buffalo say to his boy when he left for school?

A: "Bi-son."

Q: What did the ice cream say to the bowl of soup?

A: "You melt my heart."

Q: How did the boulder go to bed?

A: He rocked himself to sleep.

Q: Why did the apple go to the gym?

A: To work on its core.

Q: What do you call it when the cafeteria burns the meat?

A: A mis-steak.

Q: Why did the mittens get married?

A: It was glove at first sight.

Q: Why was the dog laughing?

A: Someone gave it a funny bone.

Q: What do you get when you combine an apple and a tree?

A: A pine-apple.

Q: Why did the toad get sent to the principal's office?

A: It was a bully-frog!

Q: Why did the scientists fall in love?

A: They had great chemistry.

Q: Why don't you want to tell jokes to an egg?

A: You don't want it to crack up!

Q: Who borrows your Rollerblades all the time?

A: A cheap-skate!

Q: What do you get when an elephant runs through the cafeteria?

A: Squash!

Q: Why did the algebra teacher break up with the geometry teacher?

A: Something just didn't add up!

Q: What do bats do in their free time?

A: They just hang out!

Q: What do mallards watch on TV?

A: Duck-umentaries.

Q: What do you do when your dog

eats your English paper?

A: Take the words right out of his

mouth!

Q: Why did the couple eat fruit for

breakfast every morning?

A: They wanted to live apple-y

ever after.

Q: Why did the baby become a scientist?

A: She liked her formulas.

Q: What did the robin do when it got sick?

A: It went to the doctor for tweetment.

Q: Why did the kid carry a dictionary in his pocket?

A: He wanted to be a smarty-pants!

Q: Did you hear about the bedbugs that fell in love?

A: They are getting married in the spring!

Q: Where do swimmers go for fun?

A: To the dive-in movies.

Q: What do you call a sheep that does karate?

A: A lamb chop.

Q: Why did the computer stay home from school?

A: It had a virus.

Q: Where did the pigs go on their honeymoon?

A: New Ham-pshire.

Q: **What do you call it when quarters rain from the sky?**

A: Climate change!

Q: **What do you call a tuna in space?**

A: A starfish.

Q: **What did the slug say when he got an A on his paper?**

A: "I snailed it!"

Q: **Why did the astronauts break up?**

A: They needed some space.

Lisa: Why did Mom buy marshmallows?

Leah: She said we needed s'more.

Q: Why did the bug hide its trophies in the closet?

A: It was a humble bee.

Q: Why did the kid put his protractor in the refrigerator?

A: Because it was 180 degrees!

Q: Why did the girl break up with the baker?

A: Because he was a weir-dough!

Q: Why did the man's jacket catch on fire?

A: It was a blazer.

Q: What is a cat's favorite vegetable?

A: As-purr-agus.

Q: Why was the chicken late for school?

A: She didn't hear the alarm cluck.

Q: Why don't you want to date a meteorologist?

A: They always have their head in the clouds.

Q: Why did the cowboy take his horse to the vet?

A: It had hay fever.

Natalee: Did you enjoy your date with the surgeon?

Cheri: Yes, he had me in stitches the whole time.

Q: What do you get when you take a picture of a plant?

A: Photo-synthesis.

Q: Why do oysters make bad dates?

A: They always clam up on you.

Q: What gets harder to catch the faster you run?

A: Your breath.

Q: What can you serve but never eat?

A: A tennis ball.

Q: What does a cow pack in its lunch box?

A: Peanut udder and jelly sandwiches.

Q: What happened when the sea lions fell in love?

A: They sealed it with a kiss.

Q: What do race car drivers eat before they race?

A: Car-bohydrates.

Q: What do you get when you cross Bambi and an umbrella?

A: A rain-deer.

Q: Why did the Skittles go to school?

A: They wanted to become Smarties!

Q: What did the baker wear on his date?

A: His new loaf-ers!

Q: What kind of shoes do butchers wear?

A: Meat loafers.

Q: Why was the insect so polite?

A: Because it was a ladybug.

Q: What happened when the janitor slipped on the wet floor?

A: He kicked the bucket!

Q: Why did the frogs get married?

A: They were toad-ally in love!

Q: What happened when the skunk wrote a book?

A: It became a best smeller!

Q: What kind of birds end up in jail?

A: Rob-ins!

Q: What happened when the library flooded?

A: It caused a title wave.

Q: Why are painters so romantic?

A: They'll love you with all their art.

Trapeze artist #1: Do you like your job at the circus?

Trapeze artist #2: I'm getting into the swing of things.

Q: What do you get when you cross a volcano and a vegetable?

A: A lava-cado!

Q: What do fish use for their lunch money?

A: Current-cy.

Q: What do you say if a porcupine gives you a kiss?

A: "Ouch!"

Q: **What kind of fish likes bubble gum?**

A: A blowfish.

Q: **Why did the crow pick up the phone?**

A: To caw, caw, caw somebody!

Q: **Why was the triangle good at basketball?**

A: It always made three pointers.

Q: Why shouldn't you date a mathematician?

A: They have too many problems!

Q: What happened to the boy who swallowed his trombone?

A: He tooted his own horn!

Q: Why don't you ever see elephants hiding in trees?

A: Because they're so good at it.

Q: Why did the jump rope get suspended?

A: It skipped school.

Q: Why did the girl have a crush on the fisherman?

A: He was quite a catch.

Mom: Do you think it will be a nice hotel?

Dad: I have reservations.

Q: Why are frogs always happy?

A: They eat what bugs them.

Q: Why can't you have class on an airplane?

A: Because your head would just be in the clouds.

Q: Why did the squirrels go on a date?

A: They were nuts about each other!

Q: Why wouldn't the sheep stop talking?

A: It liked to ram-ble!

Q: Why did the caterpillar go to so many parties?

A: It was a social butterfly.

Q: When is a mistake not a mistake?

A: When you learn from it!

- -

Q: What do you get when you cross Bigfoot and Shakespeare?

A: Romeo and Juli-yeti.

Q: What kind of clothes do dogs wear in the summer?

A: Pants.

Q: Why did the soccer player drop out of school?

A: He didn't have any goals.

Q: Why can't frogs get college degrees?

A: They croak before they finish.

Q: Why did the sharks get engaged?

A: They wanted to make it o-fish-al.

Tammy: Have you heard of the planet Saturn?

Timmy: It has a ring to it.

Q: What's a giraffe's favorite fruit?

A: A neck-tarine.

Q: Why can't elephants join the swim team?

A: They're always dropping their trunks!

Q: **Why did the boy break up with the tennis player?**

A: She made too much racket.

Lucy: How much is a pair of binoculars?

Lara: I'm looking into it.

Q: **What kind of vegetable gets a pedicure?**

A: A toma-toe.

Q: **What is a witch's favorite subject in school?**

A: Spelling.

Q: **Why did the panther break up with the tiger?**

A: She was always lion.

Q: **What do you get when you put an opera singer in the bathtub?**

A: A soap-rano!

Q: **What do you get when you cross a fruit with a rock?**

A: A pome-granite.

Q: **Why did the kid fail his survival skills test?**

A: It was too in-tents.

Q: Why don't you want to date a chicken?

A: They're cheep!

Q: Why can't you play hide-and-seek with mountains?

A: They're always peak-ing.

Q: What vegetable doesn't have any manners?

A: A rude-abaga.

Q: Where do surfers study?

A: In the board-room.

Q: When do you give astronauts their wedding presents?

A: At their meteor shower!

Q: Why are mountains always tired?

A: Because they don't Everest!

Q: What kind of bug never stops complaining?

A: A grumble bee.

Q: How did King Arthur finish his education?

A: He went to knight school.

Q: **Why did the farmer ask the florist to go on a date?**

A: It was a budding romance.

Q: **What are a horse's favorite snacks?**

A: Straw-berries and hay-zelnuts.

Q: **What kind of vegetable plays the drums?**

A: The beet!

Q: **Why was the broom late to school?**

A: It over-swept.

Q: What did the worm say to her blind date?

A: "Where on earth have you been all my life?"

Q: What do you call a boomerang that doesn't come back?

A: A stick.

Q: What kind of candy will give you a rash?

A: Licor-itch.

Q: Why didn't the branch want to play at recess?

A: It was a stick in the mud!

Q: **Why did the girl turn down a date with the sailor?**

A: There was something fishy about him.

Q: **How does a bug get around in the winter?**

A: In a snowmo-beetle.

Q: **What do you get if you cross candy and balloons?**

A: Lolli-pops!

Q: **Why wouldn't the two 4's go out for dinner?**

A: Because they already 8.

Q: Why is it a bad idea to date a firefly?

A: They need to lighten up!

Q: How does a skater cut up her steak?

A: With Roller-blades!

Q: Why did the lemon marry the lime?

A: It was his main squeeze.

Q: Why did the horse go to the guidance counselor?

A: It wasn't feeling very stable.

Q: **Why does a mushroom have a date every weekend?**

A: He's a fungi!

Brayden: Have you seen bigfoot?

Hayden: Not yeti!

Q: **What do you call a cabbage on a plane?**

A: A vegetable with its head in the clouds.

Q: **Why didn't the moon eat all of its lunch?**

A: Because it was full.

Q: What do you get when you cross a dog and a dozen roses?

A: Collie-flower!

Q: Why did the guitar player go to the auto mechanic?

A: She needed a tune-up.

Q: What is the most adorable kind of bug?

A: A cuter-pillar.

Q: What kind of dogs do they let into the library?

A: Hush puppies.

Q: Where did the cats go on their date?

A: Out for mice cream.

Q: What does an astronaut do with a bar of soap?

A: She takes a meteor shower!

Q: What is orange and sounds like a parrot?

A: A carrot.

Q: What is a boa constrictor's favorite subject?

A: World hissss-tory.

Q: Why did the potato break up with the radish?

A: He was a dead-beet.

Q: Why was the whale always painting?

A: It was art-sea.

Q: What kind of mint is bad to eat?

A: A var-mint.

Jordan: How are your scuba-diving lessons going?

Justin: Swimmingly!

Q: What did the lipstick say to the eye shadow after their fight?

A: "Let's kiss and makeup."

Q: How does a lobster like its eggs?

A: With a pinch of salt.

Q: Where do hunters like to shop?

A: Target.

Q: How did the cows get to school?

A: On a com-moo-ter train.

Q: What do you get when you cross a bike and a bouquet of roses?

A: Flower pedals.

Q: Why did the whale need a hug?

A: It was blue.

Q: What do bugs write on?

A: Flypaper.

Q: Why did the almond go to the principal's office?

A: It was going nuts!

Q: What kind of drink is never ready on time?

A: Hot choco-late

Q: Why did the baker make so much bread?

A: Because it was kneaded.

Q: What do you call a wasp that doesn't cost anything?

A: A free-bee.

Q: Why don't rivers ever run out of lunch money?

A: They're always by the banks.

Q: Why did the girl break up with the trumpet player?

A: He was always tooting his own horn.

Q: What do sharks eat for breakfast?

A: Muf-fins.

Q: When do fish swim away and hide?

A: On Fry-days!

Q: How did the bull pay for his lunch?

A: He charged it!

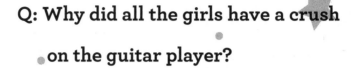

Q: Why did all the girls have a crush on the guitar player?

A: He pulled on their heart strings.

Q: Why did the driver squeeze his car?

A: Because it was a lemon.

Q: What kind of animal doesn't have a name?

A: The anony-moose.

Q: What do you call a school on a mountain?

A: A high school!

Q: **Where did the rabbits go after their wedding?**

A: On their bunny-moon.

Q: **How many skunks does it take to change a light bulb?**

A: Just a phew.

Q: **What do you call a scarecrow that follows you everywhere you go?**

A: A corn stalker!

Q: **Why did the kids get stung at school?**

A: There was a spelling bee.

Q: **When did Sir Lancelot go on a date?**

A: At knight time.

Q: **What do you get when you put glue on your doughnut?**

A: A paste-ry.

Q: **What do you get when you cross a dog and a bug?**

A: A butterflea!

Q: **Why did the car have excellent handwriting?**

A: He had fine motor skills.

Q: How did the orange make time for his date?

A: He squeezed it in.

Q: What makes a pirate angry?

A: When you take away the *P*.

Q: What kind of bug is always on time?

A: A clockroach.

Q: Why wouldn't the skeleton try to learn at school?

A: It was a numbskull!

Q: Why did the boy go hunting with his date?

A: Because it only cost him a buck.

Q: What word has three letters and starts with gas?

A: A car.

Q: What do you get when you cross a cricket and a lawn mower?

A: A grasshopper!

Q: Why did the girl need a saddle to do her homework?

A: She was horseback writing.

Q: Why did the boy want to date the professional skier?

A: She had a hill-arious sense of humor!

Q: Why did the girl join the soccer team?

A: She thought she'd get a kick out of it.

Q: Why did the book join the FBI?

A: It wanted to go undercover.

Q: Why did the girl play her drum outside?

A: She wanted to beat around the bush.

Q: Why did the fish break up with the lobster?

A: Because he was shellfish.

Q: Where do you put fish once you catch them?

A: In a cof-fin.

Q: Why was the jelly late to school?

A: It got stuck in a traffic jam.

Q: Why were the golfers eating sandwiches and cake?

A: They were having a tee party.

Q: **What is the best day to take your date to the beach?**

A: Sun-day!

Q: **Why don't crocodiles ever get lost?**

A: They're great navi-gators.

Q: **What kind of snake is good at math?**

A: A pi-thon.

Q: **What do you get if you give a robin a paintbrush?**

A: A picture that's worth a thousand worms.

Q: **Why did the girl have a crush on a skeleton?**

A: Because he was humerus.

Q: **What do a judge and a tennis player have in common?**

A: They both go to court every day.

Q: **Why aren't trees good at taking tests?**

A: They're always stumped!

Q: **How do you stop a dog in its tracks?**

A: Hit the paws button.

Q: What did the rope do after it got engaged?

A: It tied the knot.

Q: What kind of fruits do boxers eat?

A: Black-and-blue berries.

Q: What kind of bugs are good at math?

A: Account-ants.

Q: What did the meteorologist do when she broke her leg?

A: She put it in a fore-cast.

Q: **Why did the snowflakes go on a date?**

A: They were falling for each other.

Q: **What do you call a ram that tells a lot of jokes?**

A: A silly goat.

Q: **How did the brontosaurus feel after soccer practice?**

A: Dino-sore.

Q: **Why can't you win a race with a lettuce?**

A: They always have a head start.

Q: What do you get when you cross headphones and roses?

A: Earbuds!

Q: Why did the fisherman run out of money?

A: He couldn't keep his business afloat.

Q: Why did the frog join the track team?

A: It was good at tadpole-vaulting.

Q: Why was the little bean crying?

A: It wanted its eda-mommy.

Q: Why did the bird get sick after its dinner date?

A: It had butterflies in its stomach.

Q: Why wouldn't the bike wake up?

A: It was two tired.

Q: What kind of dog is never late to school?

A: A watch-dog.

Q: What does a snake like to wear?

A: Ser-pants!

Q: How did the mermaid feel when she dated a human?

A: Like a fish out of water.

Logan: I caught fifty trout with just one worm.

Megan: That sounds a little fishy!

Q: Why do the marching-band members have such clean teeth?

A: They always have a tuba toothpaste.

Q: Why was the robin eating cake?

A: It was its bird*th*-day.

Q: What did one light bulb say to the other?

A: "I love you a watt!"

Q: What is a skunk's favorite color?

A: Pew-ter.

Q: Why did the chicken join the marching band?

A: It already had two drumsticks.

Q: What is a mallard's favorite game?

A: Duck, duck, goose.

Q: What happened when the drummer fell in love?

A: His heart skipped a beat!

Q: Why did the detective fall asleep at his desk?

A: He had a pillow-case.

Q: What is a kid's favorite day of the week?

A: Fri-yay!

Q: How did the dog know its owner was calling?

A: It had collar ID.

Q: What do you call two polar bears

on a date in Hawaii?

A: Lost.

Andy: There's a skunk in my tent!

Mandy: That stinks.

Q: Why didn't anyone use the skunk's

ideas for the science project?

A: Because they stunk!

Q: What kind of batteries should you

bury?

A: Dead ones.

Q: **What happened when the pigeons fell in love?**

A: They were lovey-dovey.

Q: **Why did the girl take a blender on a hike?**

A: So she could make trail mix.

Q: **Why did the boy get kicked out of band?**

A: He always got in treble.

Q: **How did the skunk go sightseeing?**

A: In a smell-icopter.

Q: Why did the chicken break up with the rooster?

A: He had a fowl mouth!

Q: What kind of bird builds skyscrapers?

A: The crane.

Q: Why did the guitar hate going to band practice?

A: It was always getting picked on!

Janey: Do you want to look for fossils with me?

Jamie: I dig it!

Q: What did the dairy farmer say to his wife?

A: "You're my butter half!"

Q: How much did it cost to build the beaver dam?

A: An arm and a log.

Q: What did the United States say to France at midnight?

A: "Europe too late and you have school tomorrow!"

Q: Why did the banana join the gymnastics team?

A: It wanted to do the splits.

Q: Why does your grandma give the very best presents?

A: Because she's gifted.

Q: Why didn't the fisherman get his email?

A: He was out of net-work.

Q: Why don't kids in the choir get good grades?

A: They only go for the high C's.

Q: What is a tree's favorite vegetable?

A: Oak-ra.

Q: What did the horse do when she fell in love?

A: She got mare-ried.

Jerry: My campsite is better than yours!

Larry: Don't be so pre-tent-ious.

Q: Why don't fish get a summer vacation?

A: Because they're always in school.

Q: Why did the spider leave candy wrappers all over the ground?

A: It was a litter-bug.

Roger: Did you hit my car on purpose?

Roper: No, it was just a coinci-dents.

Q: Why do dragons sleep during the day?

A: They like to fight knights.

Q: What is the worst kind of candy?

A: Homework assign-mints!

Q: What do you get when you cross a spider and a computer?

A: A web-site!

Q: How do light bulbs send love letters?

A: By lamp-post.

Q: Why did the rabbit ride the roller coaster?

A: It was looking for a hare-raising experience!

Q: What is a whale's favorite thing to do on the playground?

A: The sea-saw.

Q: How did the zookeeper open the cage?

A: With a mon-key.

Q: **What time did the dentist pick up his date?**

A: Tooth-thirty.

Q: **What do rhinos and credit cards have in common?**

A: They both like to charge!

Q: **Why was the cow so popular?**

A: Because it was adora-bull.

Q: **When do they party in the castle?**

A: All knight long!

Q: What kind of flowers make great friends?

A: Rosebuds.

Q: Why did the boy wear a lampshade for a hat?

A: He felt light-headed.

Rita: Can you tell me if you brushed your teeth this morning?

Lisa: No, it's confi-dental.

Marney: What happens if bigfoot steps on your toe?

Millie: He'll Sasquatch it.

Gary: Did you see the movie about the unicorn?

Mary: I'd never myth it!

Q: Where do you find flying rabbits?

A: The hare force.

Q: Why did the kid want to study only sharks?

A: He was a fin-atic!

Q: What do you get when you combine a fish and a camel?

A: A humpback whale.

Q: Why was the nose still single?

A: It was too picky.

Q: What did the chef say after he cooked the steak?

A: "Well done!"

Q: What time is it when an elephant sits at your desk?

A: Time to get a new desk!

Q: When does a snake make you laugh?

A: When it's hiss-terical.

Q: Why did the girl break up with the astronaut?

A: He was a bit spacy.

Bob: Did you hear about the farmer who wrote a joke book?

Bill: No, is it any good?

Bob: The jokes are pretty corny!

Q: How do smart students get to college?

A: On scholar-ships!

Q: What kind of shoes do frogs wear to the beach?

A: Open-toad shoes.

Q: **What's the funniest time of day?**

A: The laughter-noon!

Q: **Why did the girl break up with the pastry chef?**

A: He kept waffling.

Q: **Why don't bakeries let their employees shave?**

A: Because they need their whisk-ers.

Q: **How do clams call their parents after school?**

A: They use their shell phones.

135

Q: Why is the baker so lazy?

A: He's always loaf-ing around.

Q: What did the buck say to the doe?

A: "I'm fawned of you, deer."

Josh: Do you think change is hard?

Joe: I sure do! Have you ever tried to

bend a quarter?

Q: What is an astronaut's favorite

part of the school day?

A: Launch time!

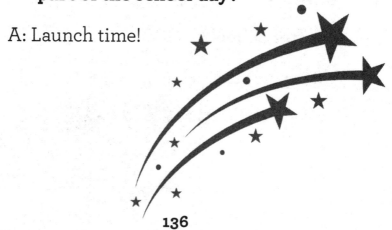

Q: What do baseball players and foxes have in common?

A: One catches fouls and the other catches fowls.

Q: Why did the girl agree to go out with the dentist?

A: She didn't want to hurt his fillings.

Q: Why don't dogs go to school?

A: They don't like arithme-tick.

Patient: Doctor, I think I broke my leg in two places! What should I do?

Doctor: Don't go to those places!

Q: Where does a bee wait for a ride?

A: At the buzz stop.

Q: What kind of bugs work at the

bank?

A: Fine-ants.

Q: What do you get if you give

diamonds to an ambassador?

A: Peace and carats.

Q: Why did the owl become a

comedian?

A: Everyone said he was a hoot!

Q: How do you know if someone ran into your car?

A: Look at the evi-dents.

Q: Where do you mail your clothes?

A: To your home ad-dress.

Q: What do you call a bottle of free perfume?

A: Un-cent-ed!

Q: How is a professor like a thermometer?

A: They both have degrees.

Q: Why did the tooth fairy fall in love with the sandman?

A: She thought he was dreamy.

Q: Why did the train go to the playground?

A: To blow off some steam.

Q: Why did the boxer punch his oatmeal?

A: He was making his break-fist.

Q: Why did the meteorologist go home?

A: He was feeling under the weather.

Q: What did George Washington call his false teeth?

A: Presi-dentures.

Q: How did the mad scientist cause a blizzard?

A: He was brain-storming.

Q: What do you call the selfie championships?

A: Olym-pics.

Q: Why did quarters start falling from the sky?

A: There was change in the weather.

Q: What did one beekeeper say to the other?

A: "Mind your own buzz-iness!"

Q: What do you call a cow doing yoga?

A: Flexi-bull!

Q: Why did the boy have a crush on the baker?

A: She was a cutie-pie.

Q: What do you call it when you pass out the cards?

A: Ideal.

Q: What's the best time to get married?

A: On a Wednesday!

Q: How do you stay happy when you're running a marathon?

A: One s-mile at a time!

Q: Why did the dog get expelled?

A: It was a pit bully!

Q: **Why did the referee jump in a puddle?**

A: He wanted to wet his whistle.

Dave: Did you like my joke about the fish?

Adam: Not really.

Dave: Well, if you can think of a better fish joke, let minnow!

Q: **Why can't fishermen get along?**

A: They're always de-baiting!

Q: **Why did the boy take the girl out for coffee?**

A: He liked her a latte.

Q: Why did the astronaut leave the party?

A: He needed some space.

Q: How do you clean a pumpkin?

A: In a squashing machine.

Stanley: What happened when you found out your toaster wasn't waterproof?

Dudley: I was shocked!

Q: How does a witch doctor stay in shape?

A: They hex-ercise!

Q: What do you get when you cross a soda and a radio?

A: Pop music!

Patient: Doctor, I think I'm turning into a piano.

Doctor: Well, that's just grand!

Q: Why did the doctor become a brain surgeon?

A: He wanted peace of mind.

Q: Why did the surfer quit her job?

A: She wouldn't get on board.

Q: Did you hear about the couple who fell in love at the Indy 500?

A: Their hearts were racing!

Q: When must you open the door?

A: When you're obligated.

Q: What does it take to work for the railroad?

A: On-the-job training.

Q: Why won't lobsters laugh at my jokes?

A: Because they're crabby!

Jenny: I should give my pig a bubble bath.

Johnny: That's hogwash!

Q: Why did the pirate share his secret treasure?

A: He wanted to get it off his chest.

Q: Why was everybody laughing at the mountain?

A: Because it was hill-arious.

Jim: I need someone to help me build an ark.

Bob: I think I Noah guy!

Q: When is a nurse an artist?

A: When she is drawing blood.

Q: Where do cows display their homework?

A: On the bull-etin board.

Q: Where does a farmer stay on vacation?

A: At a hoe-tel.

Q: What do you call soap wearing a tuxedo?

A: A detergent!

Jimmy: That soda just hit me on the head!

Bobby: Oh no, are you OK?!

Jimmy: Yeah, luckily it was a soft drink.

Q: How does the sun say hello?

A: With a heat wave!

Q: Why did the skunk have to stand in the corner?

A: It was a little stinker!

Q: What do night crawlers do before they go for a run?

A: Worm-ups.

Q: How do you feel when your shirt is wrinkled?

A: Depressed!

Tim: Hey, Mark. You want to hear my underwear joke?

Mark: Is it clean?

Q: What is a frog's favorite breakfast?

A: Toad-st and jam.

Q: Who says bad words at the store?

A: A cuss-tomer.

Q: How do you pay for the truth?

A: With a reality check.

Emma: Did you like your book about gravity?

Leah: Yes, I couldn't put it down!

Q: Where can you read about coffee cups?

A: In a mug-azine!

Q: Where can you read about insomnia?

A: In a snooze-paper.

Preston: Why did all the chickens disappear?

Winston: I don't have any eggs-planation!

Q: What do you call a book with sparkles?

A: Glitter-ature!

Q: What do you call a bunch of cows that live together?

A: A com-MOO-nity

Q: What did the mountain say to the valley?

A: "You're gorges!"

Q: What was Beethoven's favorite vegetable?

A: Bach choy!

Jenny: How was your date with the baseball player?

Jan: He knocked it out of the park!

Q: Where do heroes buy their food?

A: The super-market!

Q: **What kind of bird lives in a mansion?**

A: An ostrich!

Q: **What kind of fruit do you find in a volcano?**

A: A lava-cado!

Q: **Why couldn't the cat go on the field trip?**

A: It didn't have a purr-mission slip.

Q: **What did one woodworker say to the other?**

A: "I have a whittle crush on you!"

Q: How do you know which flag is the best?

A: You take a pole.

Q: How do you feel when a giant lizard steps on your toe?

A: Dino-sore!

Q: What's the funniest fish?

A: A piranha-ha-ha!

Q: Why was the cat afraid of the tree?

A: It was a dogwood.

Q: Where should a wildcat sleep?

A: Behind a chain-lynx fence!

Q: Why did the ape ask for lemons?

A: So it could be orangu-tangy!

Q: What do you call a cat that wants to be a nurse?

A: A first aid kit-ten.

Q: Why did the surfer go to the salon?

A: She wanted a permanent wave.

Q: How do you buy a tropical fish?

A: With ane-money!

Jane: Where did you get your backpack?

Kate: That's a purse-inal question!

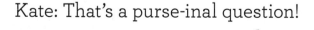

Q: What did the nurse say to the doctor?

A: "ICU!"

Q: How do you get your mom to make you some toast?

A: Just butter her up!

Q: What does a baker do for fun?

A: Bun-gee jumping!

Q: What do you get when paper towels fall asleep?

A: Napkins!

Bill: Did you like the sausage I cooked for you?

Joe: No, it was the wurst!

Q: What's a lawn mower's favorite music?

A: Bluegrass!

Q: How do you wash your stockings?

A: With a panty hose.

Q: Why did the vampire join the army?

A: So it could see combat!

Q: What do you give a dog who does extra homework?

A: Bone-us points!

Q: Why did the violin go to the gym?

A: So it could stay as fit as a fiddle.

Q: What does a baby ghost wear?

A: Bootees.

Q: What did one caramel say to the other?

A: "Let's stick together."

Q: What did the pig do when he wrote a book?

A: He used a pen name.

Q: What kind of flowers like to sing?

A: Pe-tune-ias.

Q: What happened to the singer after he was hit by lightning?

A: He became a shock star.

Q: Why did the gorilla stop eating bananas?

A: He lost his ape-tite.

Q: Why was the oak tree so proud of his heritage?

A: Because his roots ran deep.

Q: Why did the boy throw branches in the lake?

A: He wanted fish sticks.

Q: How does a bumblebee get to school?

A: On the school buzz.

Q: Why does everybody like baby cows?

A: They're adora-bull!

Q: **Why was the sailor upset over his report card?**

A: His grades were at C level.

Q: **What is a bird's favorite subject in school?**

A: Owl-gebra.

Q: **Why was the bacon laughing so hard?**

A: Because the egg cracked a yoke!

Q: **What did the sea lion say to the beaver?**

A: "Will you be my significant otter?"

Q: What is a chimpanzee's favorite drink?

A: Ape-le juice.

Q: Why couldn't the Little Pig run away from the Big Bad Wolf?

A: He pulled a hamstring!

Q: Why can't you tell a whale anything?

A: It can't keep a sea-cret.

Q: What do you call a cobra without clothes?

A: S-naked.

Q: Why did the astronaut have to write everything down?

A: He just didn't have the brain space to remember things.

Q: What has a head and a foot but no arms?

A: Your bed.

Q: What do you call a really smart bug?

A: Brilli-ant!

Q: Why is the teacher in charge everywhere she goes?

A: She controls all the rulers.

Q: Why did the beaver cross the playground?

A: To get to the otter slide.

Q: What does Miss America drink?

A: Beau-tea!

Q: What do you call a locksmith that's in a bad mood?

A: Crank-key!

Q: Why don't dalmatians take baths before their dates?

A: They don't want to be spotless.

Ken: Do you like to eat venison?

Jen: It's deer-licious!

Q: Why did the skeleton's mom tell him to eat more?

A: Because he was boney.

Q: Why didn't the eagle practice flying?

A: She thought she could just wing it!

Q: Why did the panda join the choir?

A: He had a nice bear-itone!

Q: When is butter contagious?

A: When it's spreading!

Q: What is a monkey's favorite cookie?

A: Chocolate chimp.

Q: What kind of dessert do you eat in the bathtub?

A: Sponge cake.

Cowboy #1: Get the cattle! Get the cattle! Get the cattle!

Cowboy #2: I herd you the first time.

Pete: Did you hear about the guy who invented knock-knock jokes?

Dave: No, what about him?

Pete: He just won the no-bell prize.

Q: What is a wasp's favorite hairstyle?

A: A beehive.

Q: What happened when the television crossed the road?

A: It became a flat-screen TV!

Q: Why did the koalas get married?

A: Because life apart would be un-bear-able.

Tim: Did you hear the joke about the roof?

Mark: No, what is it?

Tim: Never mind. It's over your head.

Q: Why was the man running in circles around his bed?

A: He was trying to catch up on his sleep.

Teacher: Please use a pencil for this test.

Student: What's the point?

Q: What's an astronaut's favorite drink?

A: Gravi-tea.

Q: Where does spaghetti like to dance?

A: At the meatball.

Q: What did the paper say to the pen?

A: "Write on!"

Anne: Are you sure you want another cat?

Jane: I'm paws-itive!

Q: How does an angel light a candle?

A: With a match made in heaven.

Q: What do you get when you cross a turtle and a porcupine?

A: A slow-poke.

Q: What does the Queen of England like to wear?

A: A tea shirt.

Q: What muscle never says "hello"?

A: A bye-cep!

Q: What did the glue say to the paper?

A: "I'm stuck on you!"

Q: Why was the snail too scared to leave its shell?

A: It was spineless!

Q: How many animals did Moses take on the ark?

A: None, it was Noah's ark!

Q: What do you call someone with an underwater race car?

A: A scuba driver!

Q: How do alligators give people a call?

A: They croco-dial the phone.

Jim: I have a henway in my pocket!

Joe: What's a henway?

Jim: About four or five pounds.

Sue: I finally got my new alarm clock.

Sal: It's about time!

Q: Why do monkeys like bananas?

A: They find them a-peeling.

Q: Where do cows go for lunch?

A: The calf-eteria.

Q: Why did the hot-air balloon get grounded?

A: It was getting carried away.

Q: Why was the cucumber so upset?

A: Because it was in a pickle.

Q: Why did the teacher take away the kids' soda?

A: They failed their pop quiz.

Q: What did the twig say to the log?

A: "I'll stick with you."

Q: What did the mommy elephant say to her baby?

A: "I love you a ton!"

Q: What do you call a crazy spaceman?

A: An astro-nut.

Q: How does it feel if a grizzly steps on your toe?

A: Unbearable!

Q: Why did the lettuce turn around?

A: It was headed in the wrong direction!

Q: Why did the chef quit making spaghetti sauce?

A: He ran out of thyme!

Q: Why did the orange juice get a bad grade on the test?

A: Because it wouldn't concentrate!

Q: What happened to the noodle that went down the drain?

A: He pasta way.

Q: What language do ducks speak?

A: Portu-geese.

Q: Why did the elephant quit the circus?

A: He was working for peanuts.

Q: When is music sticky?

A: When it's on tape.

Q: Where did the composer keep his sheet music?

A: In a Bachs.

Q: Why is it fun to date a farmer?

A: They're full of beans!

Q: What did the baker say to the bread?

A: "I knead you!"

Q: **What kind of bread has a bad attitude?**

A: Sourdough.

Q: **Why is bowling like a flat tire?**

A: You want a spare.

Q: **What do you get if you're allergic to noodles?**

A: Macaroni and sneeze.

Q: **What do golfers drink out of?**

A: Tee-cups.

Q: Why did the cow cross the playground?

A: To get to the udder slide.

Q: Why is it hard to have fish for dinner?

A: Because they're such picky eaters.

Q: Where do pigs keep their dirty clothes?

A: In the hamper.

Joe: Can you believe my dog caught a thousand sticks?

Jim: No, that sounds too far-fetched.

Q: Why don't dalmatians like hide-and-seek?

A: They're always spotted.

Q: What do you call an army of babies?

A: An infantry.

Q: Why did the girl break up with the butcher?

A: He was full of baloney!

Q: What do you call a shape that isn't there?

A: An octo-gone.

Larry: I dreamed about a billboard.

Lucy: I think it's a sign!

Q: Why did the spy come out at bedtime?

A: He only works undercovers.

Q: Why did the pig go into the kitchen?

A: It felt like bacon a cake.

Q: What do cats put in their iced tea?

A: Mice cubes.

Q: Why did the boy bring his piggy bank to football practice?

A: He wanted to be a quarter-back!

Q: What do monkeys eat for lunch?

A: Gorilla cheese sandwiches.

Q: Why did the music note drop out of college?

A: It couldn't pick a major.

Q: What do you get when you cross a horse and an angel?

A: A hay-lo.

Q: What can you break without touching it?

A: A promise!

Q: What has to break before you can use it?

A: An egg!

Q: Did you hear about the runner whose date stood him up?

A: His hopes were dashed!

Q: What do sailors eat for breakfast?

A: Boat-meal.

Q: Why did the monsters run out of food at their party?

A: Because they all were a-goblin.

Q: Why did the skier want to go home?

A: He was snow-bored.

Q: How does a farmer greet his cows?

A: With a milk shake.

Q: Why was the astronaut hungry?

A: Because he missed his launch.

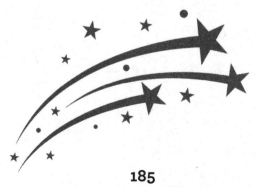

Q: Why did the beaver study astronomy?

A: It wanted to go to otter space.

Q: What did the digital clock say to his mother?

A: "Look, Mom, no hands!"

Q: Why did the boy stop carving the stick?

A: He was a whittle tired.

Valerie: Do you feel better about yesterday?

Malorie: Yes, I'm past tense!

186

Q: Why did the can stop talking to the can opener?

A: Because he kept trying to pry.

Q: What did one egg say to the other egg?

A: "All's shell that ends shell."

Q: Why did the golden retriever have a crush on the poodle?

A: He thought she looked fetching.

Lou: What happened to all your furniture?

Sue: I gave it to chair-ity.

Q: What do you call a single person who's always wrong?

A: Miss-informed.

Q: What has eighteen wheels and running shoes?

A: A truck and fielder.

Q: What do you get when you cross a rabbit and a beetle?

A: Bugs bunny.

Q: What do sheep eat for breakfast?

A: Goat-meal.

Ben: My pants almost fell down!

Ken: That was a clothes call!

Q: How did the music teacher open her classroom door?

A: She used a piano key.

Q: What kind of car do dogs drive?

A: Land Rovers.

Q: What does a golfer eat for lunch?

A: A club sandwich.

Mary: How do you feel about your braces?

Molly: En-tooth-iastic!

Q: How do you get straight A's?

A: Use a ruler.

Q: Did you hear about the soccer players who broke up?

A: They were good sports about it.

Q: When do scuba divers sleep underwater?

A: When they're snore-kling.

Q: What do you get if you scare a tree?

A: Petrified wood!

Q: Why did the horse need a suitcase?

A: It was a globe-trotter.

Bella: You should write a book!

Stella: What a novel idea!

Q: What do you call it when candy canes decide to get married?

A: An engage-mint.

Q: What do you get when you bring your fishing pole to the library?

A: You get a bookworm!

Q: What do you call a happy cowboy?

A: A jolly rancher.

Q: Why did the pony ask for a glass of water?

A: He was a little horse.

Q: Why does grass have such low self-esteem?

A: It's always getting cut down.

Q: What kind of nuts are always catching colds?

A: Cashews!

Q: What do you get when you cross an owl with a magician?

A: Who-dini!

Q: What do you call it when farmers get married?

A: Grow-mantic!

Q: Why did the banker quit his job?

A: He lost interest.

Q: What kind of boat do you hit with a stick on your birthday?

A: A pin-yacht-a.

Q: How does a pirate clean his ship?

A: With a treasure mop!

- -

Q: Where did the whales go on their date?

A: To a dive-in movie.

Q: What happened when the rabbits got married?

A: They lived hoppily ever after.

Q: Why does the queen always hold an umbrella?

A: Because she reigns.

Q: What does peanut butter wear to bed?

A: Jammies.

Diner: This soup is too bland!

Chef: That's in-salt-ing!

Q: How do you find a train that is lost?

A: Follow its tracks.

Q: What kind of fruit is never alone?

A: Pears.

Q: How do you get an astronaut's baby to sleep?

A: You rocket.

Q: Why did the squash break up with the corn?

A: It was ear-ritating!

Q: How do you spot an ice-cream cone from far away?

A: With a tele-scoop.

Q: Why do you have to keep an eye on art teachers at all times?

A: Because they're crafty.

Q: Why do your little brothers always pick on you?

A: It's their expert-tease.

Q: Where do you keep a skeleton?

A: In a rib cage.

Q: How do you call an amoeba?

A: On a cell phone!

Q: Why is everybody running around?

A: They're part of the human race.

Jeff: We're getting a brand-new scale.

Steph: I can't weight!

Miley: Do you want to go fishing with me?

Alex: That's a fin-tastic idea!

Q: How do bugs feel about summer vacation?

A: Exuber-ant!

Q: What do you get when you cross a skunk and an elephant?

A: A smelly-phant.

Q: How does a mouse open the door?

A: With a squeak-key.

Q: Why did the girl have a crush on the sailor?

A: He was easy on the aye-ayes.

Q: Why don't stars carry luggage on vacation?

A: Because they're traveling light.

Q: Where do fairies go to the bathroom?

A: In the glitter box.

Q: What do you get when you give a rabbit a sleeping bag?

A: A hoppy camper!

Q: What do taxi drivers eat for dinner?

A: Corned beef and cabbage.

Q: Why was the dentist mad at the schoolteacher?

A: He kept testing her patients.

Q: What did the beach say to the wave?

A: "Long tide no sea!"

Q: What is a unicorn's favorite vegetable?

A: Horn on the cob.

Q: What is a sheep's favorite fruit?

A: Baa-nanas.

Q: Why did the early bird need a ruler?

A: It wanted to catch an inchworm.

Q: How do pandas fight?

A: With their bear hands.

Q: What do you get when you cross a robot and a pirate?

A: ARRRR2-D2.

Q: What did the butterfly say to the ladybug?

A: "You make my heart flutter."

Q: Why can't you trust a deer?

A: They'll always pass the buck.

Q: What kind of exercise should you do after you eat fast food?

A: Burpees.

Q: When do you bring a hammer on a hike?

A: When you want to hit the trail.

Q: Why was the frosting so stressed out?

A: It was spread too thin.

Q: Why did the horse put her foal to bed?

A: It was pasture bedtime.

Q: How do you know if a joke is about your mom and dad?

A: When the punch line becomes a-parent!

Amy: Do you like your new hair color?

Ellie: Yes, I've dyed and gone to heaven!

George: I finally finished raking the yard.

James: That's a re-leaf!

Sam: Did you like your karate class?

Marcus: I got a real kick out of it!

Q: How do you fix a squashed tomato?

A: With tomato paste.

Teacher: Do you know what caused

the earthquake?

Student: I'm not sure, but it's not my

fault!

Q: What did the dogs have to eat on

their date?

A: Macaroni and fleas.

Q: What do you get when you cross a pine cone and a polar bear?

A: A fur tree.

Q: What do you get when you cross a toad and a pig?

A: A warthog.

Q: Why do sea turtles watch the news?

A: To stay up on current events.

Cassie: Do you like your astronomy class?

Kelly: It's out of this world!

Annie: I hear you got good grades in cosmetology school.

Lucy: Yes, I nailed it!

Q: Why did the cat smell so good?

A: It was wearing purr-fume.

Q: Why did the fawn put on a sweater?

A: Because it was buck naked!

Q: What do you give to a sick horse?

A: Cough stirrup.

Q: What did the horse put in its lunch box?

A: Straw-berries.

Carter: I want to have a space-themed birthday party.

Mom: Great, I'll planet!

Q: What did the stopwatch say to the clock?

A: "Don't be alarmed!"

Q: Why should you date a teacher when you grow up?

A: They have a lot of class.

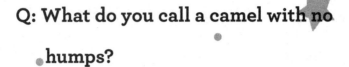
Q: **What do you call a camel with no humps?**

A: Humphrey.

Q: **What do you call a stick of dynamite that keeps coming back to you?**

A: A boomerang!

Q: **Why are forest rangers so honest and reliable?**

A: It's in their nature.

Q: **How do marine biologists feel about the ocean?**

A: They're fin-atics!

Q: Why did the boy eat waffles for breakfast, lunch, and dinner?

A: His mom said he needed three square meals a day!

Q: Why are tailors so funny?

A: They always have people in stitches.

Q: What do you call a horse in space?

A: A saddle-lite.

Q: How do you make a bug laugh?

A: Tickle it!

Q: Why do librarians move so fast?

A: They have to book it!

Q: When do sheepdogs cry?

A: When they're herding!

Q: What happened when the trees fell in love?

A: They got all sappy!

Q: Why is the shark still single?

A: It's too fin-icky!

Q: Where does a crocodile keep its milk?

A: In the refrige-gator.

Sam: Did you hear the principal wants to marry the school bell?

Joe: Yes, he gave it a ring!

Q: Does everybody drink soda?

A: It's pop-ular!

Q: What kind of dog uses a microscope?

A: A Labrador retriever.

Q: What do you call a sad cantaloupe?

A: Melon-choly.

Q: Why did the bucket go to the doctor?

A: It was looking a little pail.

Joe: Why do you always cry at lunchtime?

Bill: Because we're in the cafe-tear-ia!

Amy: Did you hear about the atoms who were dating?

Annie: Yes, but I heard they just split!

Q: What do you call a cow with a telescope?

A: A star-grazer.

Q: What kind of clothes do houses wear?

A: Addresses.

Q: What did the conductor say to the misbehaving violin?

A: "You're in treble!"

Q: Why did the girl break up with the archer?

A: He was too arrow-gant.

Q: What does a soldier wear in the summer?

A: Tank tops.

Q: What kind of shoes make fun of you?

A: Mock-asins.

Q: How does it feel to climb a mountain?

A: Ex-hill-arating!

Q: How many snails does it take to screw in a light bulb?

A: Who knows? Nobody waits around long enough to find out.

Q: What kind of animals make the best detectives?

A: Investi-gators!

Leah: Did you hear about the kid who studied to be a mime?

Emma: No, what happened?

Leah: He was never heard from again.

Q: When doesn't a lamb spend any money?

A: When it's a sheep-skate!

Q: How does a blacksmith send a letter?

A: In an anvil-ope.

Q: Why did the camel decide to take up baseball?

A: So it could be a humpire.

Jimmy: Will you give me an abacus for my birthday?

Joey: Yes, you can count on it!

Charlie: Have you ever seen a catfish?

Jerry: Yes, but I don't think he caught anything.

Q: How do you get a cat to go out with you?

A: Be purr-sistent.

Q: Why did the carpenter quit using his drill?

A: Because it was always boring.

Q: Why did the carpenter become a comedian?

A: He had a really funny drill bit.

Q: When is a rabbit's foot unlucky?

A: When you're the rabbit.

Q: What do you call a mad biscuit?

A: A hot cross bun!

Q: Why did the baker study hard in school?

A: So he could make the honor roll!

Q: How do you make a bandstand?

A: Take away their chairs.

Q: Why did the meteor do well in school?

A: It was the teacher's star pupil.

Q: What do you call a friendly scoop of frozen yogurt?

A: Nice cream!

Q: **Where did the pitcher dance with his girlfriend?**

A: At the base-ball.

Q: **Why did the rabbit go to the salon?**

A: She was having a bad hare day.

Q: **What do you get when you cross a dog and a crab?**

A: A Doberman pincher.

Q: **Why did the broccoli break up with the cabbage?**

A: It had a big head.

Q: Why did the lumberjack chop down the wrong tree?

A: It was an axe-ident.

Q: Why did the chicken go to the gym?

A: It needed more eggs-ercise!

Tim: I hope they serve fish in the cafeteria.

Mark: I'm sure they will if the fish brings lunch money.

Q: Why did the egg get kicked out of the comedy club?

A: He was telling bad yokes.

Q: What do you get when you wear a watch for a belt?

A: A waist of time!

Q: How did the moon feel after lunch?

A: Full!

Jenny: Did you hear that grandparents are invited to school today?

Josie: That's old news!

Q: How do you motivate a lazy mountain?

A: Light a fire under its butte!

Q: How do you help out a baker?

A: Make a dough-nation.

Q: Why were the shoes still single?

A: They were de-feet-ed in love.

Q: What do bunny rabbits eat in the summer?

A: Hop-sicles.

Q: Why do cannibals like dentists the best?

A: They're the most filling!

Emma: Are you allowed to write a book?

Anna: Yes, I'm author-ized.

Q: How do you hide in the desert?

A: Wear camel-flage.

Q: What do you call a can of Jell-O?

A: Gelatin.

Q: What's the coldest letter in the alphabet?

A: Iced T.

Tim: I forgot where I put my boomerang.

Scott: Don't worry, it'll come back to you!

Leah: Why do you have ten bowling balls?

Anna: So I'll always have one to spare.

Q: Why did the vegetable have to go to bed early?

A: It was just a little sprout.

Q: How did the celery get rich?

A: It invested in the stalk market.

Q: **What do you get when you bring a rooster into the bathroom?**

A: A cock-a-doodle-loo!

Q: **What did the bulldozer say to the dump truck?**

A: "I dig you!"

Q: **Why did the baker have a rash?**

A: Because he was making bread from scratch!

Q: **What do you get when you walk your dog in Paris and it rains?**

A: French puddles.

Q: What do you eat underwater?

A: Sub sandwiches.

Q: Why did the man stop at every service station on his way to work?

A: It isn't polite to pass gas.

Q: What do sailors like to read?

A: Ferry tales.

Q: Why did the bee go to the barber?

A: He wanted a buzz cut.

Dan: Can you help me find a new dentist?

Sam: You should try mine—he knows the drill!

Q: Why did the candy salesman put his phone in the freezer?

A: He had to make a few cold calls.

Josh: Let me tell you about my underwear.

Jeff: Okay, but please keep it brief. . . .

Max: What would happen if a snake swam across the Atlantic?

Jax: It would make hiss-tory!

Q: What did the bagel say to the bread?

A: "I like the way you roll!"

Travis: I was going to tell you a rumor about germs.

Scott: Why don't you?

Travis: I'm afraid it might spread.

Q: How does a deer carry its lunch?

A: In a bucket!

Q: What kind of car does the sun like to drive?

A: An S-UV.

Q: Why did the pig get out of bed?

A: It was time to rise and swine!

Q: What is E. T. short for?

A: Because his legs are so little!

Q: What do airplanes and football players have in common?

A: They both have touchdowns.

Q: Why did the bee need allergy medicine?

A: It had hives.

Q: What do you get when you cross a judge and a skunk?

A: Odor in the court!

Q: Who brings water to the baseball game?

A: The pitcher.

Q: Why did the wood fall asleep?

A: It was board.

Q: Why did the train need a tissue?

A: It was an achoo-choo train!

Q: Why shouldn't you take your date to the gym?

A: It might not work out.

Joe: Jim, does your doctor do house calls?

Jim: Yes, but your house has to be pretty sick before he'll come over.

Missy: What do you think of the Grand Canyon?

Mandy: It's gorge-ous!

Q: What do you call a stinky castle?

A: A fart-ress.

Q: Why did the boy stop using his pencil?

A: It was pointless.

Q: Why did the ruler fail in school?

A: It didn't measure up.

Q: Why did Mary's little lamb follow her to school?

A: It heard school was woolly fun.

Q: What kind of underwear does a lawyer wear?

A: Briefs.

Q: When does a hot dog get in trouble?

A: When it's being a brat.

Q: When can't you open the refrigerator door?

A: When the salad is dressing!

Parent: How was school today?

Child: There was a kidnapping in our class.

Parent: Oh, no! What happened?

Child: The teacher woke him up and gave him detention.

Q: Why don't frogs die from laryngitis?

A: Because they can't croak!

Q: How do skunks know if they're right for each other?

A: They trust their in-stinks.

Jen: Do you want to see the volcanoes in Hawaii?

Jill: I'd lava to!

Mason: Can we have a fish for dinner?

Lucas: Sure, I'll set an extra place at the table.

Q: Why was the astronaut crying?

A: He was a rocket-tear.

Q: What do you call a fake noodle?

A: An im-pasta.

Q: What has four legs but can't walk?

A: A chair.

Q: What do chickens play in the orchestra?

A: Bach, Bach, Bach.

Q: Why did the clam go to the gym?

A: To work out its mussels.

Sarah: Mom, can I plant flowers in the spring?

Mom: Yes, you May!

Q: How did the cat get the bread?

A: It baked it from scratch.

Q: Why didn't the Australian bear get the job?

A: It didn't have the right koala-fications.

Q: Why did the clock go back four seconds?

A: It was really hungry!

Q: Why did the monster get married?

A: He was the man of her screams.

Q: What is a skeleton's favorite instrument?

A: A trombone.

Q: Did you hear about the giant cow?

A: It's legen-dairy!

Q: What kind of bird is with you at every meal?

A: A swallow.

Q: What are a hyena's favorite cookies?

A: Snickerdoodles!

Q: What do you get when you cross Shakespeare and honey?

A: To bee or not to bee, that is the question.

Farmer: Why aren't my radishes growing?

Farmer's wife: Beets me!

Joel: Did you hear the joke about the strawberry jam?

Jill: Yes, it's spreading all over the place!

Q: Why did the baby snake cry?

A: Someone took away its rattle.

Patrick: Who can help me find a four-leaf clover?

Shannon: A lepre-can!

Q: What plays music in your hair?

A: A headband!

Q: What do you get when you cross a bee and a cupcake?

A: Fro-sting!

Q: Why did the hog have a stomachache?

A: He pigged out at dinner.

Q: Why did the stereo blow up?

A: It was radioactive!

Q: What did one atom say to the other?

A: "You matter."

Q: Why did they have to clean up the court after the basketball game?

A: All the players were dribbling.

Q: Why did the boy eat his homework?

A: Because the teacher said it was a piece of cake.

Q: What do you get when you throw noodles in a Jacuzzi?

A: Spaghetti.

Q: What do you get when you cross a frog and a clown?

A: A silly pad!

- -

Q: Which tree is always at the doctor's office?

A: A sick-amore tree!

Lisa: Does your dog like its flea collar?

Anna: No, he's ticked off!

Q: Did you hear about the pilots who fell in love?

A: It was love at first flight.

George: What do snowmen wear on their feet?

Henry: Snowshoes!

Q: What happens to toilet paper with good grades?

A: It goes on the honor roll!

Q: What do beavers put on their salads?

A: Branch dressing.

Q: Why don't grapes snore when they're sleeping?

A: They don't want to wake the rest of the bunch.

Q: What's a cow's favorite painting?

A: The Moo-na Lisa.

Q: What do you call a guy whose snowmobile breaks down?

A: A cab

Q: Why did the wheels fall over?

A: They were tired!

Q: What is a soda's favorite subject in school?

A: Fizz-ics!

Q: Why did the softball player save all her money?

A: She was a penny pitcher!

Q: Where do you learn to saw wood?

A: In a boarding school.

Q: Where do you wash your hands in Hawaii?

A: In the lava-tory!

Sam: How do we know carrots are good for our eyes?

Emma: Have you ever seen a rabbit with glasses?

Q: Why did the banana put on sunscreen?

A: It was starting to peel.

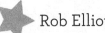
Patient: Doctor, I think I'm a chicken.

Doctor: How long have you felt like

this?

Patient: Since I was an egg.

Q: Why can't you trust a rubber

band?

A: It's always stretching the truth!

Q: Which has more courage, a rock or

a tree?

A: A rock, because it's boulder!

Q: What do you get when you cross a

dentist and a boat?

A: A tooth ferry!

Ella: Mom, have you ever watched the movie *Bambi*?

Mom: Yes, deer.

Q: Why did the girl break up with the swimmer?

A: He went off the deep end.

Q: What kind of monster never irons its clothes?

A: A wash-and-wear-wolf.

Q: What do you call someone who grabs your cat and runs?

A: A purr snatcher.

Q: How did the orange cut in the lunch line?

A: It squeezed its way in!

Sam: Why did you bring your baseball bat to school?

Cam: It's time to hit the books!

Sadie: Did you hear about the couple who fell in love on an airplane?

Susie: Yes, because love is in the air!

Q: Why did the coffee bean stay home?

A: It was grounded.

Q: What is a tree's favorite drink?

A: Root beer.

Q: Where do you take a bad rainbow?

A: To prism.

Q: What did the pepperoni say to the mushroom?

A: "You stole a pizza my heart!"

Q: Why can't you trust artists?

A: They're sketchy.

Q: Why did the baseball coach go to the bakery?

A: He needed a batter.

ROB ELLIOTT

is the bestselling author of *Laugh-Out-Loud Jokes for Kids*, *More Laugh-Out-Loud Jokes for Kids*, *Laugh-Out-Loud Animal Jokes for Kids*, and *Knock-Knock Jokes for Kids*. His popular joke books have sold more than 5 million copies. Rob has been a publishing professional for more than twenty years. He lives in West Michigan, where in his spare time he enjoys laughing out loud with his wife and five children. You can visit him at www.laughoutloudjokesforkids.com.